TRANSPARENT GOD

Poems by Claude Esteban

Translated by David Cloutier

KOSMOS
San Francisco
1982

Library of Congress Catalog Card Number: 80-84603

ISBN: 0-916426-07-6 (cloth)
0-916426-08-4 (paper)

MODERN POETS IN TRANSLATION SERIES
(Volume II)

This project was supported partially by funding from
the National Endowment for the Arts.

KOSMOS books are sewn and printed on acid free (neutral pH) paper
to ensure the integrity and long life span of each creation.

KOSMOS
381 Arlington Street
San Francisco, CA 94131
USA

Special thanks to Janet Procaccini, Susanna Lang, Kosrof Chantikian, Fernande Silverthorne and the author for their helpful and useful suggestions.

FOREWORD

Modern, as I use it in the title for this series *(Modern Poets in Translation)* does not imply simply "new" or "recent" or "original." If Picasso is modern, then so are Blake and Beethoven. If Baudelaire and Whitman, then Copernicus. No. It is not simply the "new" which is modern; something else—some pervasive element running through the works of these artists makes them modern for us: an unrelenting ingredient of transfiguration and regeneration which severs, absorbs and continues itself, which shatters, heals and then embraces itself and that emptiness from which it came—the reflection of its own gaze. The distinguishing element of the modern poem is *negation, criticism:* the power of the modern poem exists in so far as these two elements (which are identical) exist. The modern poem is also paradox, contradiction: to *negate* is to destroy, transmute, but at the same time to *continue,* the past, the world, history.

neg capability

A love poem by Sappho is a *work*, it is *living.* The modern poem is always more: it too lives but in a radically different way: it is language face to face with itself, language which rips off the mask of chatter to find that *otherness* in the world—*You.* Critical of the history into which it was born and conscious of the necessity to transmute, to transfigure this history into true reality—the *Present*—modern poetry is the regeneration of time as *presence:* this *moment, now, here, with you.*

The poem is rupture, a break in the suffocating chain of history. The modern poem is rupture and simultaneously continuation and renewal of the past. Born into the continuum of history, the poet celebrates the attempt to annul history, or at least to neutralize it, to re-create it—by returning to the beginning of beginnings, the origin of the world, return to that time when the Word was unfettered, unfragmented, when dichotomies did not exist, when Freedom & Action were inseparable.

If the infinite echo of that mutation we call *history,* its inertia of silence, residing in our minds and pockets makes us

walk slower than we would like, dissolving the living shadows
of our breath, our movement, annuling the reveries of the
touching skin; if laughter is made cripple because of the
shroud history causes to loom above and beneath our stare,
our look; and if the imagination sings with a tongue deformed
and contaminated by the barbed wire of "progress," then we
have a right to ask: How much is it possible to transmute this
history, to metamorphosize the mutilation of our senses into
a planetary sensibility, to *become what we may be:* to *Invent
Ourselves?*

This question and the insinuation it simultaneously gives
birth to are present in the work of the modern poet. The
poem, unlike prose, does not attempt to *explain* the world, it
re-creates it. This means stripping history bare into its real
form: *time.* Time in the poem is the instantaneous present,
here, now.* Time as presence is the poem. The modern poem:
language as intentionality, image, analogy: negation, criticism:
language as movement toward itself, its shadow in perpetual
pursuit of that otherness in the world—the *You*; language as
its own death and unending rebirth.

If, for Baudelaire, the poem is the analogy of the uni-
verse, it must be because the poem, through its own energy,
its own directive, continually destroys and re-creates history:
time. The poem does this by annuling at the velocity of light
the expansion and recession of history, of "progress," and
therefore time.

Sappho and Dante are not *modern* in the sense I have
just outlined because their works exist in *uncritical* time. For
the ancients time was, as Aristotle believed, periodic, cyclical,
everlasting circular motion. The winged hound of Zeus would
devour each day the liver of Prometheus—Aeschylus tells us.
Beginning with St. Augustine, this Greek conception of circu-
lar time is displaced by an unrelenting, irreversible, rectilinear
movement of history. This would continue, Augustine be-
lieved, for a finite time until that Day of days—Judgment—
brings us eternal, unchanging ecstasy or flails the human skin

---

*To learn to see to hear to say
                                    The instantaneous
Is our trade.. . . .
                                    —Octavio Paz in "Letter to León Felipe"

numb in hell. God will dissolve time; motion will swallow itself. There will no longer be death because birth will have been abolished. It is this concept of time Dante inherits and out of which he constructs the supreme architecture of his *Divine Comedy*.

The modern poem is a criticism, a destruction, a transmutation of everlasting circular time and Christian rectilinear time into the *Present*. With Blake and the Romantics, Consciousness and the Imagination are reconciled: the poem announces itself as a progression of contraries: negation and continuation, history and prophecy, dream and action. Modern poetry *comprehends time* for the first time in its authentic form: the *Instantaneous Present*. The false mask, once removed, can never again be put on. Energy becomes, is the same as, Eternal Delight.

—Kosrof Chantikian
General Editor—*Modern Poets in Translation*
San Francisco

These translations are for Anne

En parte donde nadie parecía
—Juan de la Cruz

I

Pierre
sans poids de pierre

parole écrite au livre de l'universel.

Voici
qu'une respiration
s'émeut dans la saveur des choses

et les soulève.

L'arbre, le soleil
neuf.

Comme un élancement
de la mémoire infime vers les feuilles.

Nous
au-dedans de nous. Nous, étrangers
aux portes du paraître.

Qui
nous connaît encore, qui
parle d'arracher le corps à sa contrainte —

Stone
without the weight of stone

word written in the book of the universal.

Now
a breath
stirs in the taste of things

and lifts them.

The tree, the new
sun.

Like a springing upward
of faint memory toward the leaves.

We
inside ourselves. We, strangers
at the doors of appearance.

Who
knows us still, who
speaks of tearing the body free from its constraints —

Accroître l'air, laver le souffle
de son gel, défaire
l'ombre.

Tant de matins pour
l'âme proférée —

Et le corps machinal, rivé aux
gestes qui rassurent

aux gestes noirs.

To expand the air, wash the breath
of its frost, unravel
the shadow.

So many mornings for
the offered soul —

And the mechanical body, bound to
gestures that comfort

dark gestures.

Et plus charnelle
d'avoir traversé la chair

toute pensée.

Plus forte
aussi. Eprouvant la semence
avide.
        Sachant et surmontant.

Que se relèvent
ceux-là seuls qui luttent.

Pour eux le sol
façonne la durée. Dicte sa tâche
en paraboles claires.

Ainsi consentent-ils.

Ainsi
connaissent-ils leur manque
et leur mesure.

Et la pensée travaille en eux, sans autre ciel.

And more carnal
for having passed through flesh

every thought.

Stronger
too. Testing the avid
seed.
        Knowing and surmounting.

May only those who struggle
rise up again.

For them the earth
molds the passage of time. Dictates its task
in clear parables.

And so they consent.

And so
they know their lack
and their bounds.

And thought works in them, with no other sky.

Libère le chemin, laisse
à la graine son vouloir profond. Chaque
pensée

emprisonne un peu d'ombre folle. Chaque peur
recule au fond du rêve

se retient

aux vieux désirs, aux veines
dévastées, aux
cris.

Ne cherche plus.
                    Multiples sont les voix
qui veillent dans l'obscur.

Unique
l'astre en devenir, si
haut

sur la durée.

Free the path, leave
to the seed its deep longing. Each
thought

imprisons a bit of wild shadow. Each fear
falls back into the depths of dream

clings

to the old desires, the ravaged
veins, the
cries.

Seek no more.
                    Many are the voices
that keep vigil in the dark.

Unique
the star as it unfolds, so
high

above time.

Lui, parfois.

Comme sur l'aile immodérée
du vent.

       (Nulle halte
sous le vertige
          nul ordre
qui décide de l'éclair)

Lui
souverain.

Seigneur déraciné de toute
cime.

Avec le verbe,
autour.

Seul dans le souffle.

Himself, sometimes.

As upon the excessive wing
of the wind.

         (No stopping
under vertigo
           no order
which determines the lightning)

Himself
sovereign.

Lord uprooted from every
summit.

With the word,
all around.

Alone in the breath.

Et recueillant
tout le faisceau des veines

tout l'essor des soleils qui tremblent
dans la chair —

le cœur, la vieille capitale
du désir
et de la plainte.

Sur le ciment des songes
on peut bâtir

quelque ouvrage plus pur, des citadelles
d'impossible et de silence.

Le cœur n'écoute pas. Il dit
le temps
sans interdire le travail du temps. Sans

mesurer l'usure la plus lente.

Le triomphe est ailleurs. Toute gloire
revient
à ceux qui se détournent de leur maître. Et

meurent cependant.
                    Et s'obscurcissent.

And gathering
the entire bundle of veins

the entire flight of suns trembling
in the flesh —

the heart, the old capital
of desire
and complaint.

On the concrete of dreams
one can build

some purer work, citadels
of the impossible and of silence.

The heart doesn't listen. It tells
time
without forbidding the work of time. Without

measuring the slowest degree of wear.

Triumph lies elsewhere. All glory
returns
to those who turn away from their master. And

die meanwhile.
                    And grow dark.

Mais arrachés, peut-être
à quelque langue originelle
ils vont

sans que la loi s'éveille —

foudre
enclose en un mot
pour d'autres lèvres légendaires.

Et l'air sommeille en eux
et la lueur épouse un peu leurs cendres

pour mieux nommer l'absent

celui
qui porte la parole
et la dérobe

lucide et lumineuse, altière un jour.

But torn, perhaps
from some original language
they go

no law awakes —

thunder
shut in a word
for other legendary lips.

And the air slumbers in them
and the light blends their ashes a little

to better name the missing one

the one
who bears the word
and conceals it

lucid and luminous, proud one day.

Non l'apparence

puisqu'il dissipe le vouloir d'un homme
et son vertige.

Non le passage
puisqu'il accorde l'être
avec son lieu.

Lisible entre les mots

mais évasif
aux signes qui rassemblent.

Où son ombre a décru, notre demeure.

Not the appearance

since he dispels a man's will
and his vertigo.

Not the passage
since he attunes being
to his place.

Legible between words

yet evading
the signs gathering again.

Where his shadow grew fainter, our dwelling place.

Moins l'oiseau
que l'appel.

Plus loin, les branches
se conjurent. Disent

un ciel qui monte, qui
maintient.

Ici, la terre
seulement.

Avec ses nœuds d'obscur, ses
chutes.
L'acte naissant de l'acte
et relançant
tout le moteur du jour.

L'ordre immobile.

Qu'un autre vent s'exalte, que
l'oiseau

trace le route irrémédiable.

Less the bird
than the call.

Farther on, branches
conspire. Reveal

a sky that ascends, that
upholds.

Here, only
the earth.

With its dark knots, its
falls.
The act newly born of the act
and starting up again
the entire engine of the day.

The motionless order.

Let another wind become aroused, let
the bird

trace the irretrievable road.

L'air,
entre eux. Comme

leur souffle plus serein.

Comme
un silence

immobile et qui
porterait

tout le secret du sens

par-delà
le mouvoir du monde, les mots
vides.

L'air
comme une promesse éparse. Enraciné
dans l'errance du lieu

où tout respire.

Air
between them. Like

their breath but calmer.

Like
a silence

motionless and which
would carry

the entire secret of meaning

beyond
the turning of the world, the empty
words.

Air
like a scattered promise. Rooted
in the wandering of the place

where everything breathes.

Toi qui demeures, toi
qui meurs,
            toute beauté, toute
laideur altèrent ton visage.

Nos cœurs n'ont pas voulu monter
jusqu'à ton nom.

            La soif, le vieil
espoir des choses mesurables

ont perdu le chemin, trouvé
la peur.

            Toi qui fus cette chair
première pour combattre

toi, le corps magistral, toute
candeur,

            reconnais-toi. Nous sommes
tes lointains soleils, ta

ressemblance. Notre peine
est ta peine errante. Notre mal

n'est rien que le reflet du vide
sur ta face.

            Et tout l'obscur du monde te soutient.

You who abide, you
who die,
        all beauty, all
ugliness distort your face.

Our hearts didn't want to climb
up to your name.

                The thirst, the old
hope of measurable things

have lost their way, discovered
fear.

    You who became this first flesh
so that you could struggle

you, the masterful body, all
candor,

        recognize yourself. We are
your distant suns, your

likeness. Our sorrow
is your wandering sorrow. Our wrongdoing

is nothing but the reflection of emptiness
on your face.

        And all the darkness of the world upholds you.

Dieu transparent, traverse-nous. Epuise
en nous
le devenir du sable.

L'arbre
et l'étoile n'ont pas su
grandir.
            Efface-les.

Donne à l'espace le surcroît
d'espace
                qui l'enlève. Nomme

et défais le cercle. Il
t'appartient.

Dieu vulnérable et nu dans
la tourmente
                laisse le vent te rompre.
Il te revient.

Nous, coutumiers du sol
et de l'étreinte

porte-nous sans mourir. Pénètre-nous.

Transparent god, pass through us. Exhaust
in us
the future of sand.

Tree
and star did not learn
how to grow.
                    Erase them.

Give space the increase
in space
              that lifts it away. Name

and unmake the circle. It
belongs to you.

God vulnerable and naked in
torment
              let the wind tear you apart.
It returns to you.

We, accustomed to the earth
and the embrace

carry us deathless. Penetrate us.

Dieu transparent

dieu qui consumes l'être
et le paraître.
                    Epouse le profond
de l'air.
            Parle et soutiens.

Ta mémoire
est inscrite aux voûtes unanimes. Parle
et disperse.

L'espace est une poignée d'astres dans ta main.

Lieu
antérieur au lieu. Etablissant
l'assise et l'origine.

                    Dieu matinal,
dieu murmurant, dieu de l'ouvert.

Transparent god

god who consumes being
and appearance.
                        Embrace the depths
of the air.
                  Speak and sustain.

Your memory's
inscribed on unanimous vaults. Speak
and disperse.

Space is a fistful of stars in your hand.

Place
anterior to place. Establishing
foundation and origin.

                        Morning god, murmuring
god, god of open space.

Dieu transparent

tu n'es, sans doute, qu'un sillage
plus subtil
                toute parole
éparse, loin des signes.

L'errance est ton regard. Le temps,
ce bruissement du vide

quand tu passes.

Nommer suffit
à tous ceux-là qui cherchent l'immobile.
Partager le multiple en nombres
clairs.

        Tu te détournes
de leurs jeux. Tu déconcertes leurs avoirs tenaces.

Et tu confonds leur souffle avec le vent.

Transparent god

you are, no doubt, but a more subtle
wake
      every word
scattered, far from the signs.

The wandering is your glance. Time,
this humming of emptiness

when you pass.

Naming satisfies
all those who seek the motionless.
Dividing the multiple in clear
numbers.

      You turn away
from their games. You overturn their tenacious possessions.

And you confound their breath with the wind.

Dieu transparent

dieu dévastant les mots
et le silence.

Par delà le désir, dieu
respirant.

Tu es la sève et le savoir. Tu
es le suc premier
de l'arbre.

          Dans la feuille imparfaite,
l'air mouvant.

Transparent god

god destroying words
and silence.

Beyond desire, god
breathing.

You are vigor and knowledge. You
are the tree's
primal sap.

       In the imperfect leaf,
the air moving.

Ruissellement d'étoiles
sur ta face.
            Et l'orbe entier
comme une roue qui tombe
dans ta nuit.

            Surmonter le soleil,
mouvoir l'énigme de l'immense

vers toi

vers
tout ce vide qui s'allège au loin —

Stars streaming
over your face.
            And the entire orb
like a wheel falling
into your night.

            To climb higher than the sun,
set moving the enigma of the immense

toward you

toward
all that empty space growing lighter far away —

II

Ce qui fut dit
demeure

   mais au loin.

Libre
des mots qui donnent sens. Levant
plus haut que la nécessité

la flamme de l'unique
où brûlent

l'incertain et sa loi.

Ce qui fut dit
traverse le multiple et
le rassemble.

       Sans rompre la mesure,
sans altérer ce que les heures
ont bâti.
       Pacte visible.

Avec le vide à ses côtés, comme témoin.

What was said
remains

    but in the distance.

Free
from words that give meaning. Lifting
higher than necessity

the flame of the unique
where uncertainty and its law

burn.

What was said
passes through the many and
gathers them again.

         Without breaking the beat,
without altering what the hours
built.
    Visible pact.

With emptiness at its side, as witness.

Eux,
les refuges rayonnants de l'être.

Mais ils tournent sans fin.

La parole
qui fut à l'origine

ne peut plus infléchir le sens. Chaque
lueur

intercède pour nous quand
elle est prise

en des murs de matière vive.

Eux
dorment dans leurs lois. Et la courbe
trop claire de leurs signes

traverse notre nuit sans voir, sans l'agrandir.

And they,
radiant refuges of being.

Yet they revolve endlessly.

The word
that was at the origin

can no longer inflect its meaning. Each
glimmer

intercedes for us when
caught

in walls of living matter.

And they
sleep in their laws. And the arc
of their signs, so clear

passes through our night without seeing, without magnifying it.

Inentamés, sans ombre, sans
fatigue.
      A mi-chemin de l'être
et de l'oubli.

       Qu'on les dénonce,
qu'on arrache à leurs signes
la substance.
      Ils sont la cendre
d'un ancien soleil.

Pourtant, ils ont servi.

Ils ont porté la soif et le désir
vers d'autres lèvres.
        Nommé
ce qui demeure. Ecrit
le temps.

Pour nous hausser, peut-être, hors
de nos gestes.

Pour rejoindre, au-delà, le verbe vif.

Intact, without shadow, without
fatigue.
          Midway between being
and oblivion.

               Let someone expose them,
extract the substance
from their signs.
          They are the ashes
of a former sun.

Still, they served.

They carried thirst and desire
toward other lips.
          Named
what remains. Wrote
time.

To lift us up, perhaps, outside
our gestures.

To join again, beyond, the living word.

Or nous ne sommes pas encore.

Un dieu
pourrait grandir. Il a

notre maintien, notre visage. Et
nous ne savons pas
qu'il marche parmi nous.

Un arbre le connaît. Cette branche
où le ciel s'incline.

Nous ne sommes
que nous.
        Epousant notre corps
nous pensons vivre.

Et le dieu
se fait plus modeste. S'accoutume
à décroître. Se
dérobe.
        Et dure cependant,
nous accompagne.

Nous
les fils premiers-nés de l'aube,
les errants.

But we are not yet.

A god
could become greater. He has

our manner, our likeness. And
we don't know
that he walks among us.

A tree knows him. This branch
where the sky bends over.

We are
only ourselves.
                        Marrying our bodies
we think we live.

And the god
becomes smaller. Grows accustomed
to diminishing. Escapes.
                        And yet endures,
accompanies us.

We
the firstborn sons of dawn,
the wanderers.

Sans doute, il a souffert. Connu
la haine et l'abandon.

Subi l'épreuve.

Œuvré
sans revenir au seuil.

Cette usure des yeux, ce cœur
arcbouté
contre l'informe —

                A chaque halte
un même effort de l'âme. A chaque
mot

cet appel — et la source qui s'éloigne.

Sans doute, il a faibli. Nommé
la mort
          comme la rive ultime de sa plainte.

N'écoutant plus.
Ne sachant plus comment respire en lui le Transparent.

No doubt, he suffered. Knew
hate and abandonment.

Submitted to the test.

Strove
without returning to the threshold.

This wear on the eyes, this heart
buttressed
against the formless —

                At each stop
a similar effort from the soul. At each
word

this call — and the source growing fainter.

No doubt, he grew weaker. Named
death
       as the ultimate shore of his moan.

No longer listening.
No longer knowing how the Transparent breathes
  within him.

Dieu transparent

tu ne déchires pas la nuit des corps. Tu
l'illumines.

Tu confères à l'obscur
sa qualité de source et de chemin.

Tu passes —
                    et toute chair
s'émeut parmi les songes.

Tu es le devenir du vent, sa mémoire
profonde
                    le cœur qui ne craint pas
de se soumettre et de subir.

Tu es
notre sommeil sans but
quand il aborde

à la rive antérieure, au jour promis.

Transparent god

you do not tear apart the night of bodies. You
illuminate it.

You make the dark
the very source and way.

You pass —
            and all flesh
is aroused among dreams.

You are the prospect of the wind, its deep
memory
            the heart that doesn't fear
giving in and submitting.

You are
our aimless sleep
when it lands

on the anterior shore, on the promised day.

Invente plus. Donne à l'arbre
cette saveur

dont le fruit peut s'accroître encore, cette
sève

où le soleil recouvre son pouvoir

même déchu
même arraché aux cercles de l'indiscernable.

Sois
celui qui maintient. Sois
sous les mots du jour

le mot qui dit l'assise obscure originelle.

L'autre que nous.
L'intact.

Invent more. Give the tree
this taste

so the fruit can still grow, this
sap

where the sun recovers its power

even if fallen
even if pulled from the circles of the indiscernable.

Be
the one who sustains. Be
beneath the words of the day

the word that conveys the dark original foundation.

Who is not us.
Intact.

Mais tu n'existes pas. Des mots
plus grands que nous

ont fait ton corps, ton âme transparente. Pour
nous laisser plus seuls

avec ce vide dans la voix.

Tu n'es rien. Tu es
l'ombre dont les rêves se revêtent

pour mieux nous vaincre à l'aube
et nous réduire aux phrases
de la peur.

Pourtant le nom demeure
qui t'invente. L'éclair qui te convoque. Cette
soif.
Eprouve-les. Sois le doute et l'échec. Sois
la parole insuffisante.

Traverse tout ce vide — et monte
par-delà.

But you do not exist. Words
greater than us

have made your body, your transparent soul. To
leave us even more alone

with this emptiness in the voice.

You are nothing. You are
the shadow in which dreams are clothed

to vanquish us better at dawn
and reduce us to phrases
of fear.

Yet the name remains
that invents you. The lightning that summons you. This
thirst.
Feel them. Be the doubt and the failure. Be
the inadequate word.

Cross over all this emptiness — and climb
beyond.

Dieu transparent

ton nom n'est pas à toi. Il est
opaque et lourd.

Il appartient aux choses de la terre.

Ramasse-le
dans chaque ornière du chemin. Découvre-le

sous la crevasse de l'hiver, avec
le givre.
        Branche brisée, paille
promise au feu.

Dieu transparent, il te faudra
porter

ce nom que tu ne sauras plus, ce
nom de brume.

Transparent god

your name is not your own. It is
opaque and heavy.

It belongs to the things of the earth.

Collect it
in each rut in the path. Discover it

beneath the crevasse of winter, with
the frost.
    Broken branch, straw
promised to the fire.

Transparent god, you will have to
bear

this name you will no longer know, this
name of mist.

Dieu dévasté

renonce à reconnaître
ton visage. Il

a pourri parmi les herbes. Il a
souffert

la tourbe aveugle des insectes, leurs dents
froides.

Détourne-toi.

Laisse aux racines
ces lambeaux de nuit qui te ressemblent.

Où la parole ne pénètre plus
meurt la mémoire

— la vieille guerre, aussi.

Dieu dévasté, n'écoute pas ces dieux
qui mentent.

Marche au plus près
du rien.
                    Renais en nous.

Ravaged god

give up recognizing
your face. It has

decayed among the grasses. It has
suffered

the blind mob of insects, their cold
teeth.

Turn away.

Leave to the roots
those shreds of night which resemble you.

Where the word no longer penetrates
memory dies

— the old war, as well.

Ravaged god, do not listen to those lying
gods.

Walk to the verge
of nothing.
                    Be reborn in us.

Dieu terrassé

par l'appareil ombreux, par
la blessure.

          La membrane du ciel
s'est refermée. Reste un
corps machinal
               une parole
éprise de ses lois
petites.

L'instant s'approche
où plus un mot ne franchira le seuil.

Dieu du dedans. Et tu devras
mourir
de cette mort qui monte en nous

si lente.

Tes lèvres
sont nos lèvres sèches, notre soif.

God overthrown

by the shadowy device, the
wound.

       The membrane of the sky
has sealed itself again. A mechanical
body remains
           a word
caught in its petty
laws.

The instant draws near
when no word will cross over the threshold anymore.

God within. You will have
to die
from that death which rises in us

so slow.

Your lips
are our parched lips, our thirst.

Dieu dénudé

tu as connu la mort ignoble
et solennelle
            le théâtre des cris
qui se concertent pour
haïr.

        Tu connaîtras la mort
mesquine de nos veines. Celle

qui ne dort pas. Celle qui
bouge en toute chair.

Tu descendras
par les couloirs du mauvais songe. Tu
hurleras

avec la bouche close dans le froid.

Et l'eau t'enlacera, l'eau
confuse des larmes.

Et tu seras plus nu parmi les ruines de la mer.

Naked god

you have known ignoble
and solemn death
                    the theatre of cries
orchestrated for
hate.

        You will know the paltry
death of our veins. That

does not sleep. That
stirs in all flesh.

You will descend
through nightmare corridors. You
will howl

with your mouth shut in the cold.

And the water will embrace you, the confused
water of tears.

And you will be more naked among the ruins of the sea.

Dieu dépouillé
dieu que le vent déchire —

Nous t'avons rencontré, au bord
des routes, dans
le soir.

      Lorsque le cœur
n'est plus
          lorsque les yeux cherchent
plus loin que leur fatigue

et luttent mal
contre le mur aveugle, le
malheur.

Nous t'avons reconnu. Mais
nous voulions un dieu plus magnifique.

Comme une terre
neuve
où nous déprendre de nos soifs.

Tu n'avais rien. Tu nous offrais
le pain des misérables.

Nous t'avons oublié. Nous
n'avons pas voulu nous reconnaître
en ton regard.

Stripped god
god the wind rips apart —

We've encountered you, by
roadsides, in
the evening.

When the heart's
no more
when eyes search
farther than their weariness

and struggle feebly
against the blind wall,
misfortune.

We recognized you. But
we wanted a more magnificent god.

Like a new
land
where we could leave our thirsts.

You had nothing. You were offering us
the bread of the wretched.

We have forgotten you. We
didn't want to recognize ourselves
in your glance.

Dieu traversé
            non par la lance
obscure ou le blasphème

— par notre peur charnelle. Dieu
qui meurt.

La vérité
n'habite pas le corps, mais
l'exaspère.
            Elle a besoin
de ces lambeaux qui brûlent pour
grandir.

Aussi faut-il
qu'un dieu l'éprouve dans ses veines. Avec

le fer, avec le feu plus pur.

Là où le sang
jaillit

surgit la source encore
et la semence.
            Là où le ciel s'effondre

un autre ciel
déchire l'horizon, flambe à la cime.

God pierced
            not by the dark
lance or blasphemy

— by our bodily fear. God
who dies.

Truth
doesn't live in the body, but
exasperates it.
                It needs
these rags that burn
to become greater.

A god too must
test this in his veins. With

iron, with pure fire.

There where the blood
spurts

the source springs up again
and the seed.
                There where the sky gives way

another sky
tears the horizon apart, blazes up to the summit.

Dieu des chemins

nous t'avons poursuivi
jusqu'aux frontières de l'absence.

Par-delà la lumière et l'ombre, sans
pouvoir
même toucher le seuil

ou ce qui fut ton nom, jadis, sur d'autres lèvres.

Dieu des matins

nous t'avons provoqué
avec des mots obscurs, des mots
patients.
            Nous t'avons confondu, seigneur
des routes, avec nos craintes.

Tu nous voulais joyeux, dociles
entre tes doigts.

God of paths

we have pursued you
to the frontiers of absence.

Beyond light and shadow, without
even being able
to touch the threshold

or what your name was, once, on other lips.

God of mornings

we have provoked you
with dark words, patient
words.
        We have confounded you, lord
of roads, with our fears.

You wanted us joyful, docile
between your fingers.

Etoilement parmi les signes
de l'espace.
                    Flamme
au-delà des feux.

Voici que chaque mur
vacille
            et cherche l'ombre informulable
pour survivre.

Un astre — et le matin
s'accroît.
                    Une pensée

— et la houle l'emporte vers sa gloire.

Le ciel n'a pas failli.

Libre le cœur, légitime
soudain
l'usure dans l'immense.

Starlight amid the signs
of space.
        Flame
beyond fires.

Now each wall
trembles
        and seeks the informulable shadow
to survive.

A star — and the morning
expands.
        A thought

— and the wave carries it toward its glory.

Heaven has not failed.

The heart free, legitimate
suddenly
the wearing down in the immense.

Sable qu'un peu de vent
soulève

et qui revient, qui
se rassemble infime au pied des arbres.

Ne craignez plus. Ne
fuyez pas ce qui sépare.

L'air
fut le maître unique. Et qu'il nous chasse,
grain par grain

est la marque de son amour
sans lieu

— sa main prodigue.

        Sand that a little wind
lifts up

and returns, gathers
minute at the foot of trees.

Fear no more. Do not
flee what separates.

The air
was the unique master. And that he hunts us,
grain by grain

is the mark of his
placeless love

— his lavish hand.

Arbre du sens

avec ton germe toujours
neuf

le miel futur parmi les claires
feuilles bourdonnantes —

Tu t'éloignes
de nous.
Tu regagnes le règne
incorporel.

Tu brûles dans le vent de l'insubstance.

Tree of meaning

with your seed always
new

    the future honey among the clear
buzzing leaves —

You go away
from us.
        You regain the incorporeal
kingdom.

You burn in the insubstantial wind.

III

Mais tout
s'arrête ici. Les mots

le bruissement de l'âme sur les lèvres.
Même l'air

comme un bloc de gel entre des mains.

Qui
demeure debout, qui
frappe encore à la muraille du silence —

Lui
le seul à pouvoir prétendre

s'est perdu.

Tout
tombe. Et le soleil

revient. Trouve la terre à nu. Scrute
l'espace.

But everything
stops here. Words

the soul's murmuring on the lips.
Even the air

like a block of frost between hands.

Who
remains standing, who
still beats against the high wall of silence —

He
the only one able to pretend

has lost himself.

Everything
falls. And the sun

returns. Finds the earth naked. Scrutinizes
space.

Terre
entravée.

Ciel qui s'étouffe entre
ses branches.

Un dieu mortel
s'attache à la paroi. Pèse
plus fort

contre l'écorce opaque de la cendre. Cœurs
maçonnés.

L'air
au-delà. Verbe du vent.

Vacance de l'impondérable.

Earth
trammeled.

Sky choking between
its branches.

A mortal god
clings to the wall. Weighs
heavier

against the dark crust of ash. Hearts
walled-in.

Air
beyond. Word of wind.

Emptiness of the imponderable.

Sommeil du sens. Monde
amassé en sa matière
aveugle.

Mur minéral.

Nul ne se lève encore.
Forçant la route.

La parole
est trop loin. Le feu

perdu
par-delà les silex, dans
la mémoire.

Reprendre au premier mot.

Dénouer
le serpent des signes.

Sleep of meaning. World
amassed in its blind
matter.

Mineral wall.

No one rises up yet.
Forcing the road.

The word
is too distant. The fire

lost
beyond flint, in
memory.

To recover the first word.

To untangle
the serpent of signs.

Or ils persistent par-delà. Domaines
de haute mer.

Langages
que le vent convoque.

Nés avec nous. Mais sans
le corps nocturne
qui harcèle.

Attentifs au soleil de l'être.
Inassouvis.

But they persist beyond. Domains
of the high sea.

Languages
the wind convenes.

Born with us. But without
the tormenting nocturnal
body.

Attentive to the sun of being.
Unappeased.

Vagues signes du ciel.

Et la terre
alentour

ne sachant plus garder les choses
qui l'honorent.

La terre —

avec ses doigts rompus. S'attachant
à la chair des songes.

    Tombant
toujours.
      Jusqu'à l'abîme
du non-dit.

L'enfer est là. Table du monde
insubstantielle.

Relief du rien — où tous les corps
s'épuisent
        sans un cri.

Vague signs in the sky.

And the earth
all around

no longer knowing how to hold the things
that honor it.

The earth —

with its broken fingers. Clinging
to the flesh of dreams.

      Falling
always.
        Down to the abyss
of the unsaid.

Hell is there. Insubstantial
plain of the world.

Hill of nothingness — where all the bodies
are worn away
             without a cry.

Lui, l'emmuré.

Lui dont les mots vacants ne savent
dire

en nous comme au dehors
de nous

rien
que la nuit.

Lui, au plus près de ce qui
dure sans espoir.
                              Lui, notre usure.

S'accoutumant

aux ruses de la soif, à
l'air qui manque.

He, the walled-in one.

He whose vacant words do not know
how to speak

inside us as outside
us

nothing
but night.

He, closer to what
endures without hope.

                     He, our wearing away.

Growing accustomed

to the ruses of thirst, the
lack of air.

Rien que l'hiver.

Ici
le feu
recule dans les pierres.

Dieu dénudé, il te faudra marcher
sur tout ce gel.

Nothing but winter.

Here
the fire
retreats into the stones.

Naked god, you will have to walk
over all this frost.

Dieu dévorant la sève
et la substance.

Dieu voleur de l'été, dieu
consumant le corps
avec l'esprit.

Voici que tu reviens
à nous.
          Tu nous appelles
avec des mots qui
tremblent.

              Tu n'as plus de regard, plus
de visage, mais ta main

s'attache à notre main, demande
encore le feu
le pain

réclame, emporte.

Dieu miséreux, dieu ténébreux, dieu
sans merci.

God devouring the sap
and the substance.

Thieving god of summer, god
consuming the body
with the spirit.

Now you return
to us.
        You call to us
with words that
tremble.

            You have no gaze, or
face anymore, but your hand

clings to our hand, still
asks for the fire
the bread

calls for, carries off.

Destitute god, shadowy god, god
without mercy.

Dieu qu'on écrase sous le pas, sous la poussière
de l'oubli

dieu sans visage.

Dieu qui sommeille dans la plaie, dieu qui déchire
et disparaît, dieu
misérable.

Dieu démuni, dieu dévasté, dieu de tous ceux qui tombent.

Dieu plus mesquin que le mépris, dieu
trop petit pour être dieu

dieu sans miracle.

Dieu sans témoin, dieu sans appui, dieu sans parole.

Dieu
de l'atroce et de l'effroi, dieu de la honte
et de la nuit, dieu sous la terre.

Dieu dans le sel et dans la soif, dieu confondu, dieu
répandu.

Dieu dans les larmes.

God one crushes underfoot, under the dust
of oblivion

faceless god.

God who sleeps in the wound, god who tears apart
and disappears, miserable
god.

Deprived god, ravaged god, god of all those who fall.

God more paltry than scorn, god
too small to be god

god without miracle.

God without witness, god without support, god without word.

God
of atrocity and terror, god of shame
and night, god under the earth.

God in the salt and in the thirst, confounded god,
scattered god.

God in tears.

Nous te perdrons.

Nous
marcherons

jusqu'à ce que ta mort s'efface.

Nous guérirons. Nous
laverons nos lèvres dans l'oubli.

Nous passerons.
                    Et tu seras
ce peu de terre qui
demeure.
                    Vieil ossement
du sol.

Plus dur que nous.

We will lose you.

We
will walk

until your death is obliterated.

We will heal. We
will wash our lips in oblivion.

We will pass on.
                    And you will be
this bit of remaining
earth.
          Old bones
of the soil.   *Yeats: rag e bone shop*

Harder than us.

Ta parole, comme
le blé.

Largesse des lointains, folle
moisson après les heures
lentes.

L'hiver a tout repris.

La fatigue et la faim, les deux
compagnes

ont travaillé longtemps, dressé la table, ouvert
le seuil.
                    La nuit les a chassées. Leur
bouche s'est emplie
de cendre.

Ta parole, plus seule — avec
le vent.

Your word, like
wheat.

Bounty of the distances, wild
harvest after slow
hours.

Winter has recovered all.

Weariness and hunger, two
companions

have worked a long time, set the table, opened
the doorway.
Night drove them away. Their
mouths filled
with ash.

Your word, more alone — with
the wind.

Puis un nom fut lancé, le
tien

pour qu'au delà des choses déclinantes
un seul amour soit dit.

Toi
et l'envers de toi. Tout mouvement

épris de l'avenir et
du retour
            sans que la durée bouge
entre les deux montants
de l'immuable.

Rien que ce nom, le tien. Et l'âme
inentamée du monde
                    — ta mémoire.

Then a name was thrown, your
own

    so that beyond waning things
a single love might be spoken.

Yourself
and the inverse of you. All movement

in love with the future and
the return
         without the moment shifting
between the two poles
of the immutable.

    Nothing but this name, your own. And the unbroken
soul of the world
          —your memory.

Et tu t'approcheras. Tu
poseras

ô dieu chantant, la main sur notre épaule.

Tu chasseras
la peine. Tu voudras

que ce jour soit le premier jour
parmi les choses.

Tu nommeras le monde — et
il sera

lui l'incertain
comme un arbre qui bruisse après l'orage.

Et nous serons plus clairs

ayant maintenu l'ombre et le chemin
de l'ombre

sans faillir.

And you will approach. You
will place

oh singing god, your hand on our shoulder.

You will drive away
sorrow. You will wish

this day to be the first day
among things.

You will name the world — and
it will be

uncertainty itself
like a tree rustling after the storm.

And we will be clearer

having upheld the shadow and the way
of the shadow

without fail.

Pour qu'une autre intercède.

L'autre, la voix
du sol.

Celle qui monte
avec la houle des fourmis. Fragile
et forte.

Ignorée du soleil, captive
des couloirs.

Libre soudain. Toute
levée
contre l'incandescent.

Lucide. Nue.

So another might intercede.

The other, the voice
of the soil.

The one who climbs
with the surge of ants. Fragile
and strong.

Unknown to the sun, captive
of passageways.

Free suddenly. Lifted
entirely
up to the incandescent.

Lucid. Naked.

— Je suis la route et le matin. Je
suis l'hiver
quand il éclaire tout le gel des branches.

— Je suis le soir et le chemin. Je
suis l'été
sur le sommeil des fruits. Je suis

la terre succulente.

— Je te connais, dieu murmurant. Je
suis la bouche qui
t'annonce.

— I am the road and the morning. I
am winter
when it illuminates all the frost on the branches.

— I am the evening and the path. I
am summer
on the sleep of fruit. I am

the succulent earth.

— I know you, murmuring god. I
am the mouth that
announces you.

Une pierre a vibré. Sous
l'arbre substantiel

tout un peuple s'émeut. Parole
obscure.

Ne tarde plus.

L'air progresse et
parvient.
             Le ciel profère
une candeur.

Tout l'imparfait s'évade vers la cime.

A stone reverberated. Beneath
the substantial tree

an entire people are roused. Dark
word.

Delay no more.

The air goes on and
arrives.
        Heaven speaks
simply.

Everything imperfect escapes toward the summit.

WORKS BY CLAUDE ESTEBAN

Poetry

La saison dévastée, Galerie Jacob, Paris, 1968.
Celle qui ne dort pas, Paris, 1971.
Croyant nommer, Editions Galanis, Paris, 1972.
Dans le vide qui vient, Maeght éditeur, Paris, 1976.
Terres, travaux du cœur, Flammarion, Paris, 1979.
Cosmogonie, Lettres de Casse, Draguignan, 1981.

Essays

Chillida (monograph on the sculptor), Maeght, Paris, 1972.
Veilleurs aux confins, Fata Morgana, Montpellier, 1978.
L'immédiat et l'inaccessible, Editions Galilée, Paris, 1978.
Un lieu hors de tout lieu, Editions Galilée, Paris, 1979.
Palazuelo (monograph), Maeght, Paris, 1980.

Translations

Le singe grammairien by Octavio Paz, Skira, Geneva, 1972.
Más allá by Jorge Guillén, Maeght, Paris, 1974.
Cantique by Jorge Guillén, Gallimard, Paris, 1977.
Poèmes parallèles / (Góngora, Quevedo, Aleixandre & others),
    Editions Galilée, Paris, 1980.

CLAUDE ESTEBAN was born on the twenty-sixth of July 1935 in Paris. He has published five volumes of poetry and has translated widely from the Portuguese, Italian, Spanish, and Catalan. From 1973 to 1981 he was Editor of the poetry review *Argile*. *Transparent God* is his second collection of poems in English. *White Road: Selected Poems of Claude Esteban,* translated by David Cloutier, was published in 1979 by the Charioteer Press (Washington, D.C.). He presently teaches Spanish Literature at the Sorbonne.

DAVID CLOUTIER is the author of four volumes of poetry: *Soft Lightnings* (Copper Beech, 1982), *Tongue and Thunder* (Copper Beech, 1980), *Tracks of the Dead* (Blue Cloud, 1976) and *Ghost Call* (Copper Beech, 1976). In 1980, his versions of Siberian, Eskimo and Northwest Coast Indian songs appeared under the title *Spirit Spirit: Shaman Songs.* His translation of *The Beaches of Thule,* poems by the contemporary French poet Jean Laude, will appear in the Autumn of 1982 published by *KOSMOS.*